BIRD NOTES

poems by

Betsy Hughes

Finishing Line Press
Georgetown, Kentucky

BIRD NOTES

Copyright © 2017 by Betsy Hughes
ISBN 978-1-63534-332-8 First Edition
All rights reserved under International and Pan-American Copyright Conventions.
No part of this book may be reproduced in any manner whatsoever without written permission from the publisher, except in the case of brief quotations embodied in critical articles and reviews.

ACKNOWLEDGMENTS

These poems have appeared in other publications, some with minor changes:

"At the Edge of Appalachia Preserve" and "Snowy Owl" in *Poems from the Far Hills*, Wright Library Poets
"By the Conowingo Dam" in *Common Threads*, 2016
"Nocturnal Vision" in *Mock Turtle Zine*, issue 10
"Phoenix" in *Best of 2016*, Ohio Poetry Association

These poems first appeared in my book *Breaking Weather*, winner of the 2013 Stevens Poetry Manuscript Competition, National Federation of State Poetry Societies Press, 2014:

"A Fragile Grace"
"Ballet Lesson"
"Cardinal Truth"
"Loon"

Publisher: Leah Maines

Editor: Christen Kincaid

Cover Art: Jasmine Al-Masri

Author Photo: Adam Al-Masri

Cover Design: Elizabeth Maines McCleavy

Printed in the USA on acid-free paper.
Order online: www.finishinglinepress.com
also available on amazon.com

Author inquiries and mail orders:
Finishing Line Press
P. O. Box 1626
Georgetown, Kentucky 40324
U. S. A.

Table of Contents

Northern Gannets 1
Scintillissima 2
At the Edge of Appalachia Preserve 3
By the Conowingo Dam 4
In the Park 5
Snowy Owl 6
Loon 7
A Murder of Crows 8
Nocturnal Vision 9
Phoenix 10
Guilt 11
Ballet Lesson 12
Marginalia 13
Cardinal Truth 14
The Indigo Macaw 15
Forest Songs 16
A Fragile Grace 17
A Question of Disparity 18
The Aviary 19
Avianoid 20
Birds of Prey 21
Lost Bird 22
Arrival at Kitty Hawk 23
Ornitheology 24

*in memory of my father
Lawrence Mills
who loved birds*

NORTHERN GANNETS

They gather high above the white-capped sea,
above the cliff tops, under Scottish sky.
The gannets spread their wings to guarantee
a striking six-foot span. They beautify
the scene, then tuck in their extensions, drop
and slice into the water, keen as knives
or arrows, spearing fish without a stop
as they pursue and pin by power drives.
Their vision is binocular, and eyes
positioned to determine distance, chests
conformed to cushion impact. Such surprise
and confidence in their descents and quests!
I cannot fathom how they dive so deep
or how they dare to plunge from heights so steep.

SCINTILLISSIMA:
Smallest of the Smallest Species of Bird

Above the flower, hovering with flair,
it vibrates, flaps its wings at reckless rates
and frequencies so high the sound—a dare—
becomes a hum. *Huitzil* it creates.
The acrobat flies backward, upside down,
it pirouettes and playfully pursues
an evanescent path in dancer's gown
so gossamer that light and air suffuse
the little body of the stirring bird
which measures merely this: two inches long.
For moments it has paused and softly whirred
and winged its own distinctive humming song.
Like bees it seeks its sweets from floral gifts;
it drinks the nectar, turns away, uplifts.

AT THE EDGE OF APPALACHIA PRESERVE,
Adams County, Ohio

These Caribbean tropicals must face
the treacheries of raptors on their way;
they migrate north until they reach this place
where for their mating season they will stay.
Now see them sweeping up in giant arcs,
then swooping in descent upon the trees.
Observe that prairie warbler who embarks
upon his coupling enterprise with ease.
Bright yellow paints his underside, and he
is handsome, topped with streaks of olive green.
Attracting there upon a cedar tree,
he shakes the feathers on his tail: Convene!
He sings a high-pitched *zee-zee-zee-zee-zee*;
his lovebird soon will hear this melody.

BY THE CONOWINGO DAM

On bended knee, with vantage from the ground,
the still photographer was posed in prayer;
his camera ready, he without a sound
anticipated drama in mid-air.
The fish were jumping in the water's spray
just where the dam let loose its overspill.
He watched them frolic in their fatal play
and waited for the timing of the kill.
As if on cue, descending from the sky
the bird of prey dived suddenly to pierce
into the scaly flesh and satisfy
a law of nature—beautiful and fierce.
Photographer and raptor, eagle-eyed,
both seized the perfect moment to decide.

IN THE PARK

He talks philosophy to pigeon friends
who flock to him for wisdom in the crumbs
he spreads for them; he never condescends,
attends to them as eager equals—chums.
What can be said? What language can be heard?
He nods, they nibble while they bob their heads.
He mutters word, they speak in solemn bird,
partaking their communion crusts of bread.
What can be known? What politics resolved?
He needs their company, they need his food.
This microcosm, mutually involved,
is peaceful and companionable and good.
Both parties know exactly how to share,
engaged in conversation on the square.

SNOWY OWL

The birders measure your enormous span
of wings: your spread of five feet wide is rare.
They marvel how a migratory plan
can guide an owl through miles and miles of air.
All memory of lemmings, Arctic prey,
has vanished in these far Ohio fields
where, fearless, hunting openly by day,
you locate other predatory yields.
I know your stolid stance upon the pole
will change within an instant when your eyes
unlid their yellows to detect a vole;
then you will pounce and take it by surprise.
I keep my distance, stunned by snowy white.
You keep your wary watch in winter light.

LOON

This creature seeks the lonely Northern lakes,
seclusion in lagoons of Arctic cold;
the company of others it forsakes.
        I'll not go there for long—I am not bold.
This bird's sleek body is designed to dive,
its bill is dagger-shaped to catch the fish;
so deep below it feeds to stay alive.
        I'll not drop down to drown—I fear the wish.
Uncanny ululation echoes near,
a mournful lunacy which must appall,
bizarre, demented laughter without cheer.
        I'll not stay here—I hear my own strange call.
Inside the lovelorn weirdness of this tune,
I wonder: Am I crazy as a loon?

A MURDER OF CROWS

I hear them utter their distinctive call
that summons others with a raucous caw,
then see them mob, descend to ground to maul
a little rodent, watch them eat it raw.
Soon air is shaking with the whir of wings
which cut through wind and flutter on my roof,
unloosing evil spirits, demon things
with glossy blackness, beak and devil hoof.
I tell myself they're really only crows
but sense a wraithlike presence, dark, perverse,
beyond the ceiling—there—which hovers, grows,
and causes me in fear and awe to curse.
My superstition may be more macabre
than bird behavior. Hear the murder throb.

NOCTURNAL VISION

If humans have evolved from ancient apes,
can birds descend from dinosaurs I ask
as, slipping into dreams of scaly shapes,
I let my sleep's unconsciousness unmask
whatever horrors haunt me in the night
and, shuddering, surrender to my fears
of whirring bats (phantasmagoric sight!),
of bestial fowl (swooping overseers!),
of hideous Harpies (terrible and black!),
hallucinations in a Hitchcock show
preparing for an avian attack
which may occur before I, waking, know
I am not prey, and specters fly away,
while dark devolves into the light of day.

PHOENIX

I caused this conflagration, I'm to blame,
not you, whose temperature became so cool;
I fanned this blaze, I cannot tame the flame,
my reason has departed, I'm the fool.
Your passion has been spent, but I still burn
with aching ardor, unrequited zeal;
although you spurn me, yet my heart must yearn
for what we had, for fantasy so real.
Now let the fire purge me and consume,
and watch my cinders gather all around;
among stoked embers some live coals will bloom
like flowers for another day newfound.
Then from my ashes I will surely rise
into new being, ready for surprise!

GUILT

I wonder at your wide outspreading wings,
the power of your long and graceful bill!
When Nature shows me such amazing things
why must I curse the creature, must I kill?
Am I so frightened by the feathers' white?
Does your pure beauty cause me such chagrin
that it incites my anger, I must smite
your innocence?   Is this my jealous sin?
Until I learn the answers I must wear
the burden of the bird around my neck;
you are the woeful cross I have to bear,
reminding me to hold my pride in check.
I am responsible. This is the code.
But, Albatross, you are a heavy load.

BALLET LESSON

The flow has ebbed and left a tidal pool.
A little tern wades in with webbed feet
so delicate they wobble in the cool
but keep the balance of this athlete.
She moves her slender body, takes the stance
of ballerina on the sandy floor,
performs her birdlike steps in daring dance
just inches from the deeper waters' shore.
Encore! Petite danseuse with such esprit
that you forget the dangers of the flood,
the predators that spoil your fantasy,
the squalls and everything that makes you scud.
Oh graceful swallow, from you may we learn
through time and tide to turn and turn and turn.

MARGINALIA

At water's edge the lovely ibis wades
upon his stilts in perfect balance, tall,
while dragonflies in iridescent shades
spread out their fragile wings in gauzy shawl.
Adjacent to the formal garden grow
neglected plants and grasses in the wild,
whose floral beauty, not designed for show,
is unarranged and natural, not styled.
Beside the highway lies less-traveled road
digressing into pathways which, untried,
provide more meaning and a different mode
for noticing the wonders on each side.
The fringe contains the crucial little things
which coil into consciousness with springs.

CARDINAL TRUTH

This landscape has two hues, just red and white,
a crested finch with scarlet plumage bold
upon the snow, so bright and stark a sight
that its heraldic message must be told.
Behold this cardinal, with blood of life,
alone, flamboyant on a field of fleece,
now boasts its color, knows no cause for strife
in this hibernal wonderland of peace.
This vivid bird, however, warns of war:
A drop of ruddy paint, if bled, would shed
on innocence that glistens on the floor
hoar-frosted, pristine pure. Its stain could spread.
Potential life or death in this tableau:
the cardinal all red against the snow.

THE INDIGO MACAW

From "Memento Vitae," an ekphrastic response to Isabella Kirkland's Stilled Life

The tapestry is rich, for every hue
arrests the viewer, who observes in awe:
a large exotic bird in luscious blue;
      (So beautiful this indigo macaw!)
a lion tamarin with golden head;
a giant comet moth in vivid lime;
the veins of various stems in vital red;
      (A bright display of nature's paradigm!)
the verdant vegetation everywhere
which grows to camouflage the lizard's green;
a radiated tortoise resting there;
an orange pitcher plant; (Amazing scene!)
These flora, fauna, rendered crystal clear,
could these abundant species disappear?

FOREST SONGS

The loggers knew their call in predawn mist
and stopped the noisy timber saws to hear
the voices of these fog larks, ocean-kissed,
Keer keering on the Oregon frontier.
Each year the marbled murrelets would nest
on branches of the Douglas fir, where moss
would make a covered platform for their quest
to nurse a single egg, before the loss
of coastal old-growth conifers, a threat
to their secure and hidden habitat.
Now we must be confronted with regret,
refuse to yield or pray requiescat,
preserve some woods which have not yet been cleared,
and save some creatures not yet disappeared.

A FRAGILE GRACE

Now can you hear the huia's final song,
will its lament continue to be heard?
This elegy is protest against wrong.
Beloved by Maoris was New Zealand's bird!
Now can you see the huia's frantic flight,
its silhouette against a heaven's hue?
Without escape from deadly human sight,
thus once it flew, then vanished from our view.
Now must you know the lesson that it brings—
that nature's balance, delicate to keep,
demands our care. This special species wings
to us a message with a truth so deep:
A creature, beautiful, with fragile grace,
can soon meet an extinction without trace.

A QUESTION OF DISPARITY

His eye is on the sparrow, so they say.
Some try to think that this may be, and I
am gratified to have the rich supply
of happy fortune that has come my way,
the clothing, food, and shelter every day
that nourish and sustain me, fortify.
But there are more deserving creatures. Why
disparity?   I ponder in dismay.
Theology can't answer or explain
why Providence protects the favored few,
while others, left defenseless, hungry, gaunt,
like sparrows scratching in the ground for grain,
abandoned, harrowed, and denied their due,
are chained in hopeless poverty and want.

THE AVIARY

The woman in the wheelchair watched the bird
inside the dome of glass. Was it a finch?
Some years ago she would have known the word
which whirred inside her head. She did not flinch
to see the blood upon its fragile wing,
for she had also flown against hard walls,
this Home enclosing her from everything
that might hold freedom from such songless halls.
Still bleeding, then it pecked the floor for seed.
She mouthed its hunger in her soundless shout,
for captured there was something of her need
which understood the ageless *Let Me Out!*
The aviary was a cage-in-cage;
she wheeled away in empathy and rage.

AVIANOID

Composed of several carbon fiber sticks,
a whir of wire, sensors, microchips,
and Mylar wings, it does amazing tricks.
Our wildest dreams it craftily outstrips!
It flies off noiselessly when launched in air,
behaves so much like nature's bird, alive,
that once a hawk attacked it, unaware,
and caused the robot's rare unprogrammed dive.
With four-foot wingspan, weight less than a pound,
and airborne longer than propellered drone,
it threatens and it promises profound
effects upon the world that we have known.
While Robo Raven hovers unopposed,
will covert information be disclosed?

BIRDS OF PREY

The women heard the news and found the shack.
With furtive looks they waited by the bed
and held their dreadful vigil, dressed in black.
They witnessed breathing stopped and body dead.
Without a pause, one gave the cheek a peck
before she grabbed a string of homemade beads
which hung invitingly around the neck
and satisfied her hungry, ruthless needs.
Another snatched a saucepan from the stove
and danced a stolen broom around the floor.
The scavengers scooped up their treasure trove
before departing through the unlatched door.
So vultures feed, they plunder and they take.
Beware their grievous greed, their gruesome wake.

LOST BIRD

About a sense of hope I reminisce.
When I recall its presence, I can smile
until I am aware of what I miss:
A bird once perched within my soul awhile.
The wind is not beneath its wings today.
Instead my spirit droops in breathless air,
the sky is gray where hurtful hawks hold sway,
the grip of grief is suffocating there.
Tomorrow will my feathers lift me high,
away from sorrow wing toward free frontiers,
relieved of burdens, resurrected fly,
this phoenix burned, consumed, then washed by tears?
Although I think I'll find my song again,
sometimes my doubt descends, I wonder when.

ARRIVAL AT KITTY HAWK

We wondered whether it would still be there,
our beach, familiar Carolina coast,
when suddenly we sniffed the salty air
and knew it was within our reach, almost.
Almost! But first we climbed the grassy dune,
a hill so high we could not see the sea.
Soon all would be revealed to us, and soon
our summer, oceanside, would set us free.
Yes, free to shuffle barefoot on the sand
or wade in wild water, realize
our Outerbanks adventures on the strand
while we explored new worlds of rich surprise.
You're here! The ring-billed gulls with welcome squawked.
We're here! We flew with wings, no longer walked.

ORNITHEOLOGY

Imagine there's a station in the sky
where birds fill up on special ethered air,
an atmosphere so rarefied they fly
inebriated with the truths they dare,
descend to our location here on earth
(where hopeless humans laboring below
with futile feuds and wasteful wars, a dearth
of inspiration in a scene of woe),
refuel us—creation taking place,
a mediation under feather-fleece
of music we can, pumped to full, embrace,
uplifting, winging to a world of peace.
Believe that harmony exists—Birdsong!
The miracle was in us all along.

NOTES

"Scintillissima"
   The Aztec god Huitzilopochti is often depicted as a hummingbird. "Huitzil" describes the sounds of the hummingbird's wing beats.

"The Indigo Macaw"
   This all blue Brazilian parrot is one of the rarest parrots in the world. Classified as Endangered, it has suffered from habitat loss, hunting and trapping for the aviary trade.

"A Fragile Grace"
   The huia was a species of New Zealand wattlebird. It became extinct in the early twentieth century, primarily as a result of overhunting and widespread habitat destruction. The huia held a special place in Maori culture; the bird was regarded as sacred, and the wearing of its skin or feathers was restricted to people of high status.

With an abiding passion for poetry, **Betsy Hughes** graduated from Vassar College, earned her M.A. in English from The University of Dayton, and taught English for thirty years at The Miami Valley School. In retirement, she has moderated courses in literature, creative writing, and the arts for The University of Dayton Osher Lifelong Learning Institute. Her appreciation for poetry continues to be nourished by her writing friends in the Wright Library Poets and the Dayton Poetry Circle, as well as the Ohio Poetry Association and Ohio Poetry Day.

Betsy Hughes was winner of the 2013 Stevens Poetry Manuscript Competition sponsored by the National Federation of State Poetry Societies. *Breaking Weather* was published by the NFSPS Press in 2014. Her poems have also appeared in the *Society of Classical Poets Journal, the Mad River Review, Mock Turtle Zine*, and several anthologies published by the Ohio Poetry Association, including the recent ekphrastic anthology *A Rustling and Waking Within.*

Betsy is fascinated by the sonnet genre because of its inherent qualities of sound and rhythm and its wedding of discipline and freedom. Many of her sonnets relate to nature, as in this collection. Others employ the traditional form for contemporary subjects, with special focus on environmental, social, and political issues.

www.ingramcontent.com/pod-product-compliance
Lightning Source LLC
LaVergne TN
LVHW041515070426
835507LV00012B/1584